The Dog Made Me Buy It!

written and designed by

ALICE L. MUNCASTER & ELLEN SAWYER

PHOTOGRAPHY BY PETER BASDEKA

CROWN PUBLISHERS, INC.

NEW YORK

To Lady and Baby,
our first dogs

Published by Crown Publishers, Inc., 201 East 50th Street, New York, New York 10022
CROWN is a trademark of Crown Publishers, Inc.
Manufactured in Hong Kong

Book design by Alice L. Muncaster and Ellen Sawyer

Library of Congress Cataloging-in-Publication Data

Muncaster, Alice L.
     The dog made me buy it / by Alice L. Muncaster and Ellen Sawyer.

     p. cm.

         1. Dogs in advertising.   I. Sawyer, Ellen.   II. Title.
HI-5827.M873   1990
659.1′96367′009—dc20   89-27022
                                                            CIP

ISBN 0-517-57453-5

1   3   5   7   9   10   8   6   4   2

First Edition

A Treasury of Dogs Who Sold Yesterday's Products

hat made you buy the kind of soap you always use? Why did you select that box of breakfast cereal? How did you choose the brand of gasoline you prefer?

Whether or not we like to admit it, advertising influences our purchasing decisions. And, although it's not the only factor we consider when we buy something, advertising helps us choose between one product and another.

That's where dogs come into the picture, and that's what this book is all about. Dogs—and advertising. The canine connection is real, and through the pages of this book, you'll see how advertisers of the past put dogs to work helping to sell all kinds of products.

Of course, there are many modern products that also feature dogs in their advertising or make use of a "spokesdog." But it's easy to turn on the television and see a dog in a commercial. Or pick up a magazine and, chances are, you'll find a dog pictured in an ad for film, beer, or, most typically of all, dog food.

So we selected mostly antique advertising for this book. The items shown on these pages are generally from before 1930. They are beautiful and rare examples of dogs in the advertising spotlight. Many are more than a hundred years old. These would not be easy to find, and most people would not be able to see them anywhere else.

As you turn the pages, you'll probably ask yourself, "Why dogs?" The reason is rooted in human nature. People like animals, and people are attracted to pictures of animals almost as readily as they are to real animals. Advertising research experts say dogs and cats, along with

In the 1880s and 1890s, manufacturers used colorful cards like this one to advertise their products. Dressed-up animals acting like people were popular during this late-Victorian period. The J. & P. Coats thread company created several sets of charming cards that were eagerly collected by their customers.

babies, outrank almost all other subjects for attention-getting power. And being noticed is the first step toward the all-important "purchase decision."

Since the earliest of times, when dogs first began to share space with people, they have been considered a friend of mankind. Dogs have faithfully followed their human benefactors, rewarding kindness with affection and proving their understanding of our needs by offering companionship, unconditional love, and the valuable service of protecting property and loved ones from harm. So it's easy to see why people would respond to a dog in an ad. It's a familiar sight and a pleasant one for almost everyone.

If you've read or heard about our other books, you may think of us as strictly "cat people." It's true that we have written three books about *cats* in advertising (*The Cat Made Me Buy It!*, *The Cat Sold It!*, and *The* Black *Cat Made Me Buy It!*). But we love dogs, too. And we found the advertising of the past that featured dogs was so interesting and unusual that we wanted to share that with you as well. So, while some people think of

themselves as only a "cat person" or a "dog person," we found ourselves to be both. And we've found good reason to think you don't have to be a dogs-only person to appreciate the images found in this book.

As you browse through the pages, you'll notice some recurring themes. We found that dogs were most often pictured as "man's best friend," a watch dog or guardian, a child's companion; along with other pets (especially cats); or in a hunting scene. These situations may seem to be stereotypes today, but remember, you're looking at the kinds of images that actually helped create those stereotypes in the first place. They weren't necessarily such familiar ideas fifty to a hundred years ago, when these advertisements were new!

One kind of dog you won't find in this book is the dog that became famous through movies or television. Although such canine stars as Lassie and Rin Tin Tin did their share of product endorsements, we've concentrated for the most part on the "underdogs"—the dogs we discovered symbolizing the family pet or the dog that inspired a slogan for a particular product.

The bloom of health again rests on the cheeks of our darling, thanks to PARKER'S TONIC

Children and pets share a special bond of love, captured on this late–nineteenth–century advertising card from Hiscox & Co. of New York. Parker's Tonic, introduced in the late 1870s, was said to revitalize diseased blood and cure such diverse ailments as rheumatism, malaria, colds, nervous stomach, and insomnia.

This ad was one of a series for Mansion Polish in which pets held conversations about the condition of the house before or after Mansion Polish was used. It appeared in British magazines in the 1930s. Mansion Polish was first sold in 1912 and is still available today in England.

There were all kinds of dogs that helped sell a wide variety of items, including food, clothing, magazines, household goods, tobacco, and medicines. Products were sometimes named for a particular breed of dog. Some ads pictured a champion—a winner of blue ribbons in several dog show competitions—perhaps to associate the idea of being "top dog" with their product. Some companies even went so far as to use an illustration of a dog as the corporate logo.

From advertising calendars to package labels, magazine covers to outdoor signs, dogs definitely made people sit up and take notice of them and the products they spoke for. Moreover, since many of these products are still sold today, we think you'll agree that "pooch power" can be pretty effective. As salesmen, we rate these dogs a howling success. Or maybe the cat's meow!

"Die-cuts" were sometimes used as advertising devices in the late 1800s. Printing companies lithographed colorful images on cardboard that were automatically cut into shapes during the printing process by a type of punch-out tool called a die. A space was usually left blank for imprinting the name of an advertiser—such as The White Shoe Store, shown here.

Before modern plastic wrap and storage containers were routinely used in the kitchen, stoneware crocks, jugs, and canisters were popular with cooks. This brightly lithographed tin sign would have hung in a store or restaurant supply company to promote the use of stoneware. This sign was produced by the American Art Works Company of Cochocton, Ohio, one of the premier advertising lithographers from 1909–1950. The dog shown pestering his friend for a bite of doughnut appears to be an Irish terrier.

uster Brown charmed a generation of readers and left a tremendous imprint on American merchandising.

Along with his dog, Tige, Buster Brown was originally the star of a comic strip created by R. F. Outcault. Outcault is considered the father of the modern-day comic strip because he was the first cartoonist to feature continuing characters with dialogue included right on the art panels.

The first Buster Brown strip appeared in 1902. Two years later, Outcault set up a booth at the St. Louis World's Fair and sold the licensing rights for the use of Buster Brown and Tige to a variety of businesses. Today, this is common business practice, but in 1904 it was a brilliant stroke of marketing genius. Outcault thus allowed Buster and Tige to appear on product packages and customer giveaway items for such diverse products as shoes, socks,

bread, spices, cigars, and whiskey.

The Buster character was a mischief-maker, but each comic strip story ended with a moral—a bit of sermonizing that left children with a sense of right over wrong. It is said that Outcault's own dog was the model for the Tige character.

So popular was the comic strip that a whole generation of boys were nicknamed Buster, and many early twentieth-century families had a dog named Tige. Buster's haircut is even today known as a "Buster Brown cut." The style of his clothing and sailor hat became generically known as a "Buster Brown outfit," and in many parts of the country, people buying children's shoes of the buckle-and-strap style simply asked for "Buster Browns"—no doubt to the delight of the Brown Shoe Co. of St. Louis, an early licensee that still produces the brand.

The last Buster Brown comic strip appeared in 1926, and Outcault died in 1928.

The Brown Shoe Co. kept the image of Buster Brown and his dog, Tige, before the public's eye with heavy promotion of the logo and name. The decal above could be placed on a mirror or on the front door glass of a shoe store. The image also appeared inside the company's Buster Brown brand of children's shoes. The advertising card on page 8 is a rare example of a "mechanical" card. When the tab is pulled, the boy's mouth opens and the dog's eyes move—just the sort of novelty giveaway that would make customers likely to remember the Buster Brown brand name.

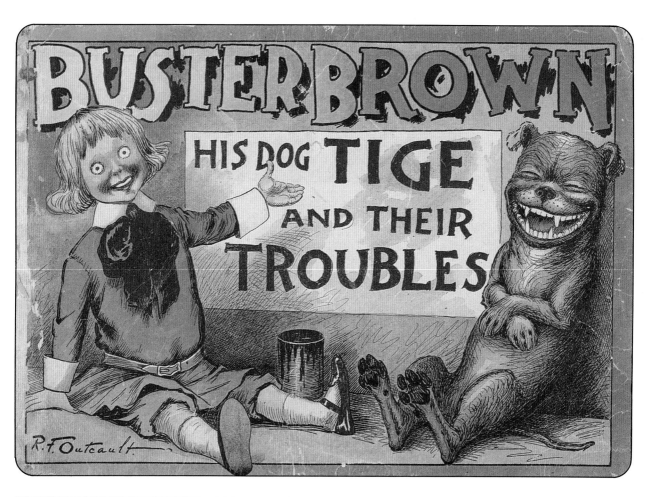

Buster Brown was so popular that all sorts of companies paid the cartoon character's creator for the right to use the boy-and-dog image on their products. Good examples are the spice tins (*left, bottom*) from a St. Louis company and the cover of a story book (*left, top*)—one of a series that entertained children in the early years of this century. The beautiful label below was on the inner lid of a box of thirteen Buster Brown cigars. The box was trimmed with tape showing the same scene. The cigars also came packaged in a lithographed round tin container showing the same illustration. The artist customized both packages, however; the tin was featured in the illustration on the tin, while the cigar box was pictured on this cigar box label.

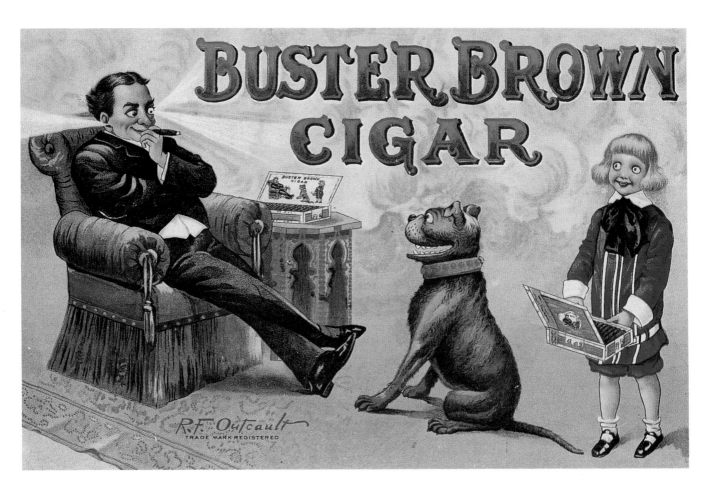

The image of a large sturdy dog helped the Northern Coal & Dock Co. promote its "heating champion" Great Dane coal. The company was doing business in Minnesota as early as 1905 but was incorporated in Ohio in 1906. Its last year of business was 1950. This cardboard dealer sign, measuring 15″ high × 20″ wide, is from the 1930s, when coal furnaces heated most of America's homes.

Products bearing the 666 brand name were used as early as 1897 by sufferers of colds, headaches, and even malaria. In the 1930s, a series of advertising fans featuring characters from Greek and Roman mythology was created to promote the 666 name. The goddess of the hunt, Diana, is shown here with a sleek Art Deco–style greyhound as a tie-in to the ad slogan. Today, the Monticello Drug Co. still makes 666 products.

The J. & P. Coats thread company advertised thread to American women of the late 1800s with advertising cards featuring children and animals in whimsical settings. Because of the beautiful illustrations, cards were eagerly saved to look at again and again. The card at the top, from 1881, lists fifteen sewing machine brands in a chart on the back. The correct Coats' thread and needle numbers for each are shown, according to the type of sewing to be done—from coarse to fine. Coats' major competitor was George A. Clark, maker of Clark's threads. Eventually, the two companies merged to form what is now Coats & Clark, Inc. Coats & Clark threads are still produced today.

Dogs in Great Britain around 1915 may have behaved as well as the one shown here if they were washed with Jeyes Dog Soap! The small tin box shown above featured the colorful "washday" scene on the top; inside were four bars of Jeyes soap. The soap was made through the mid-1930s. Today, Jeyes Group produces bleaches, detergents, and other household products.

THE HOME FRIEND
AND ILLUS MECHANICS

THE HOME FRIEND MAGAZINE
Established 1904

ILLUSTRATED MECHANICS
Established 1913

Vol. XXXIV, No. 9

DECEMBER, 1937

PLEASE SANTA give them only to GOOD BOYS and GIRLS

"Belated Christmas"

A Beautiful Christmas Story With An Inspiring Message

Children often consider their pet to be their best friend. So it's not surprising to find variations of this theme used by the publication shown at the left and by the food manufacturer who produced the can shown below. *The Home Friend* was a general-interest publication containing fiction and even a do-it-yourself section. It was published in Kansas City, Missouri, and the warmth of this Christmas cover is as timely today as it was in 1937. The Friend's brand was actually a product of the Friend Brothers company of Boston, Massachusetts, but the charming can label literally illustrated a friendship theme. Although no longer produced, the beautiful label (ca. 1930) no doubt attracted shoppers to the Friend's brand on store shelves for many years.

ipper, a British fox terrier born in 1884, is perhaps the most recognized dog in advertising. He was fond of nipping ankles but was a wonderful pet to his owner, artist Francis Berraud, who created an oil painting of Nipper listening to a cylinder phonograph (ca. 1890).

Berraud adapted the painting to show an updated disc record player and sold it to the Gramophone Company of Britain in 1899, where it was used to advertise that company's products. By 1900, the U.S. rights to the Nipper image were acquired, and Nipper was being used to promote records and phonographs made by the Victor Talking Machine Co. of Philadelphia.

In 1929, the Radio Corporation of America (RCA) acquired the Victor company and continued using the Nipper symbol. In fact, Nipper is often called "the RCA dog" even today.

Nipper was a well-known symbol in the U.S. and abroad—one of the few corporate logos to be widely accepted into popular culture. The Gramophone Company installed a Nipper-shaped weather vane atop their headquarters building in England in 1911. Four stained-glass Nipper windows were added to the Victor Cabinet Factory in Camden, New Jersey, in 1915. By 1921, Victor offered reproductions of the famous Nipper painting as a sales tactic, and the original oil painting was displayed in New York in 1952 when "His Master's Voice" LP records were introduced. And in 1984, a plaque commemorating the real Nipper's final resting place—77 Clarence Street, Kingston, Surrey, England—was erected.

Today, the Nipper symbol belongs to Thomson Consumer Electronics (RCA) of Indianapolis, Indiana.

The Victor Talking Machine Company used the instantly recognizable Nipper symbol on its records. This label is from a single-sided 78-rpm record made before 1923.

Nipper was so popular that the American Lithographic Co. of New York created the "His Master's Choice" cigar brand in 1904. It was transferred to the Wing Cigar Co. of Columbus, Ohio, in 1907. Charles M. Wing continued manufacturing cigars and other tobacco products until 1917. The lithographed tin shown below is from that period and held fifty cigars when it was new.

Around 1910, when this spice container was produced, there were more than twenty spices in the Gillies product line. So a kitchen of the early 1900s could have been guarded by a number of these serious dogs looking down from the spice shelf! Each Gillies container featured the face of the same dog, but no one knows what connection this image had to the company's owners. The company was founded in 1840 when Wright Gillies, a young clerk in a tea store in New York, opened his own coffee roasting business. Gillies retired in 1884, but his brother and their descendents continued the business until 1947, when it was sold. Today, the Gillies Coffee Co. offers a wide variety of specialty coffees and teas to the retail and restaurant trade, but the spices are no longer made.

Grape-Nuts cereal was originally created by C. W. Post as a health food. It was baked into a hard cake, then crushed to produce a distinctly crunchy breakfast food. Since the original recipe is still used today, Grape-Nuts tastes the same now as it did in the early 1900s, when the beautiful tin sign shown at the right was produced. This image was also used in Grape-Nuts magazine advertising for a number of years.

Whether this dachshund was dreaming of a future victory or basking in the glow of a recent win, no one can tell! But readers of *Woman's Home Companion* in 1939 could delight in the sentiment all the same, for Americans have always enjoyed winning in competitions—from county fairs to World's Fairs. This magazine was one of the most popular women's publications for sixty years (1897–1957). The cover illustrations were known for depicting charming scenes of home and family life.

When there's a choice of pet foods available, it's often the brand with the best advertising that wins the sale. These unusual old lithographed tin signs represent advertising at its best—especially to dog owners! Melox and Melox Marvels dog foods were made by W. G. Clarke & Sons, Ltd., Limehouse, London.

A Cat and a Dog were wedded one day,
Together, people said they would not stay,
But Puss was quite wise, and instead of a bone,
She fed him on bread which was made from Yeast Foam.

Before radio, television, and movies, a great number of families turned to music and song to while away the hours. So two well-respected piano manufacturers produced these cute doggie die-cuts to gain attention for their brands in the late 1800s. The Shaw Company originated in Erie, Pennsylvania, in 1895 and, though acquired by a Baltimore firm in 1890, produced pianos under the Shaw name until 1915. The Sterling Company dates to 1866 in Derby, Connecticut. The company first manufactured organs, exclusively, but by 1896, the booming factory was operating at peak capacity—producing sixteen pianos and ten organs per day! Thirty years later, however, as silent movies and speakeasies of the Roaring '20's abounded, Sterling went out of business—a victim of America's changing tastes in entertainment.

"Opposites attract" might explain how a dog and cat could set up housekeeping together on the dealer advertising card shown at the left (actual size). Dressed-up animals were a kind of novelty illustration popular with Victorian America, so the Northwestern Yeast Co. of Chicago showed good marketing sense when they featured these humanized pets to promote their yeast product to consumers in 1900. While customers admired the front of this card on display at a grocery or general store, only the store owner saw the message on the back, which assured dealers that even though Yeast Foam carried a premium price, customers preferred it to the hundreds of less expensive but inferior brands of competitors. Yeast Foam was introduced in 1880; the Northwestern Yeast Co. went out of business in 1947.

This lovely advertising card from 1892 captures a familiar scene of friendship between a child and the family pet. The E. W. Hoyt Co. of Lowell, Massachusetts, created a series of beautiful advertising cards featuring children and animals and was one of the earliest prolific users of such cards. Rubifoam, a tooth polish, is no longer produced, but Hoyt's German cologne is still made by the J. Strickland Co. of Memphis, Tennessee. Many superstitions accompanied European immigrants to America in the late nineteenth and early twentieth centuries. Although the origin of the custom is unknown, wearing Hoyt's German cologne is still considered good luck!

When Furchgott's department stores of Jacksonville, Florida, ceased operation in 1985, it was the end of a retailing story over a century old. The first Furchgott and Brothers store opened as a dry goods establishment in tiny quarters in the late 1860s. Several partners and name changes later, the company became known simply as Furchgott's and grew into a chain of quality department stores. This cute advertising die-cut was made in 1883, after Charles Benedict was associated with the firm and Morris Kohn joined the company as senior partner.

OLD FAITHFUL
MARCH & TWO-STEP
BY
ABE HOLZMANN
5
PUBLISHED BY LEO FEIST NEW YORK

In the early years of the twentieth century, the piano was often the most treasured piece of furniture a family could own. Since there were no television sets or radios, and phonographs were still somewhat of a novelty, most people relied on the piano for entertainment. Music publishers produced sheet music, like "Old Faithful," shown here, and people who could follow the notes on the piano could generally count on being the center of attention with family and friends. The publisher of this sheet music from 1907 undoubtedly chose a dog for the cover illustration because dogs are known to be devoted and loving pets.

One way advertisers of the past could keep their name before customers was to give them calendars. And when the illustration was as beautiful as this child with a puppy, they could be assured it was saved all year—and beyond! The Excelsior Stove and Manufacturing Co. was already well known in the early 1900s for its Excelsior stove brand but went to great lengths to promote its National brand as well. National stoves took top honors in competition at the St. Louis World's Fair of 1904, a fact the company included on its calendars, advertisements, and sales literature for years to come. The Excelsior Stove and Manufacturing Co. continued to produce stoves in Quincy, Illinois, until 1956.

Over the years, an exceptionally large number of bulldogs have been pictured in advertising. The most interesting of these also bear the Bulldog name.

The breed is said to date back to the time of the ancient Greeks. But it wasn't until the late 1800s and early 1900s that bulldogs really became popular in the United States. That was the end of the Victorian era, and the British were fond of the breed. At the time, whatever was fashionable in England quickly found its way into vogue in America, where large numbers of English immigrants had settled.

Despite a somewhat ferocious appearance, bulldogs are known as intelligent, even-tempered pets that are good with children. So any company that chose this dog's name and image—particularly around the turn of the century—did so both to associate its product with the bulldog's reputation as a courageous guardian and to take advantage of a popular trend in pets!

Bulldogs were found on sheet music and magazine covers. There were brands of household cleaning products that pictured bulldogs on the label—including scouring powder and even lye! And the phrase "bulldog grip" was used in advertising for dental products, jar lids, and garters.

During World War I, British soldiers gave the nickname "Bulldog" to the American-made Mack truck because of its reputation of being strong and durable. Today, huge Mack trucks still ride the U.S. highways and their figural bulldog hood ornaments are a familiar sight.

Today, although there is not the widespread use of bulldogs in advertising that there once was, bulldogs remain a popular breed in Europe and America.

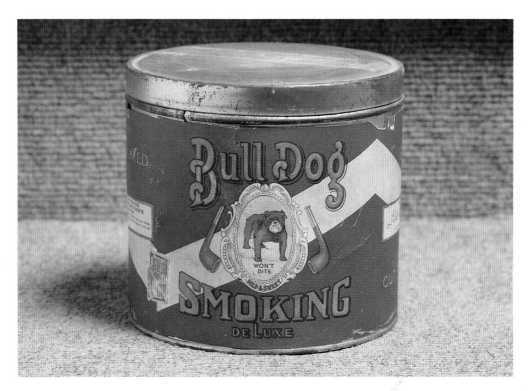

"Won't Bite" was a widely used slogan for Bull Dog smoking tobacco, as shown on this colorful tin container. The Lovell-Buffington Tobacco Co. of Covington, Kentucky, made the Bull Dog brand famous, along with another variety—Bull Dog Twist for chewing— in the late 1800s and early 1900s. The company, founded in 1864, was an independent manufacturer that survived national depressions, union labor difficulties, and fierce competition from the large tobacco conglomerates known as the Tobacco Trust before it went into receivership in 1917. By 1922, the company had ceased operations.

Among the ways the Lovell-Buffington Tobacco Co. promoted the Bull Dog brand was by making match holders available, such as the one shown at the right, which could be given to customers where the brand was sold. These were then hung in kitchens, where the matches came in handy for lighting wood stoves. William Specht, whose name appears on the holder, was a rancher who began operating a Bulverde, Texas, country store in 1899. Specht's store carried general merchandise, including groceries, clothing, and hardware. A cotton gin and a bar could be found on the premises as well. Specht's son, Richard, bought the store in 1921 and continued its operation under the Specht name until 1961.

Before modern pesticides were invented, flies and other insects made themselves right at home more often than most homeowners could tolerate. Although dozens of anti-insect products were available in the late 1800s and early 1900s, few were actually effective. So the Frank Laboratories of Cincinnati, Ohio, at least made their product *look* tough by picturing a bulldog and naming their insect powder after the breed. The dog on the lithographed tin container demonstrates how the small package (*inset*) was to be used—pierce the top and shake or squeeze the powder out. Although no records can be found for the company, the packages are of the type made around 1880–1910.

Suspenders were a fashion necessity for men in the early 1900s. Bull Dog suspenders were highly advertised by Hewes & Potter of Boston, Massachusetts, and the unusual countertop display (*below*) would have been draped with suspenders and used in a general store or department store so customers could see for themselves that the Bull Dog brand was strong and well made. Many of the Bull Dog advertisements also featured the bulldog trademark. The example at the right is from around 1906. Although suspenders are making a comeback today, the Bull Dog brand is no longer available. James A. Hewes and Frank W. Potter started the company in 1890; Hewes & Potter, Inc., was dissolved in 1968.

Airedale brand cigars were named in honor of a real dog. The brand was introduced in 1913 by Charles C. Thompson, who owned a pet airedale at the time. Because there were so many cigar brands manufactured in America in the late 1800s and early 1900s, it was important to differentiate brands with colorful box labels. Labels were created and customized by enterprising lithographers who sold them to manufacturers, distributors, and stores. C. C. Thompson and his brothers, E. S. ("Star") and Russell, together with C. G. Price, owned and operated a chain of wholesale cigar and tobacco stores in the southern United States. The Thompson Brothers and Price Cigar Co. went out of business around 1925.

Patent medicines were popular in the late nineteenth century, when antibiotics and vitamins were not yet available. Doctors, chemists, and pharmacists experimented with combinations of roots and herbs to create tonics for every sort of illness. The C. I. Hood Co. of Lowell, Massachusetts, produced Hood's Sarsaparilla, an early patent medicine that was promoted as a remedy for indigestion, poor appetite, colds, and tired blood. This advertising card is from before 1900.

During the 1920s, when the First World War was over and men had again turned their thoughts toward fashion, Kuppenheimer was a name they turned to for stylish menswear. This advertisement, which appeared in *The Literary Digest* of October 27, 1923, made a "gentlemanly" statement about the company and the dapper Kuppenheimer brand clothing. Today, Kuppenheimer Men's Clothiers is a subsidiary of the Hartmarx Corp. and operates more than a hundred retail clothing stores.

September MONTHLY

Listening in

The American Magazine (*right*) showcased American home life of the 1920s. Since puppies are a natural part of any domestic scene, they are an appropriate subject for this 1924 cover. *The American Magazine* began in 1876 as *Frank Leslie's Popular Monthly*, filled with short stories, recipes, poetry, and essays. By 1905, after several name changes and editorial switches, *The American Magazine* emerged, with an emphasis on scandals in politics and big business. But when the Crowell Publishing Co. purchased the magazine in 1915, it returned to home-oriented articles; profiles of successful, hard-working Americans; and fiction stories, a positioning it continued throughout the 1920s. *People's Popular Monthly* (*left*) was published from 1896 to 1931. Although it first emphasized articles about current events, by the time this winsome cover appeared in 1923, it had become a household magazine for women. Both covers were created by artist Warren Davis.

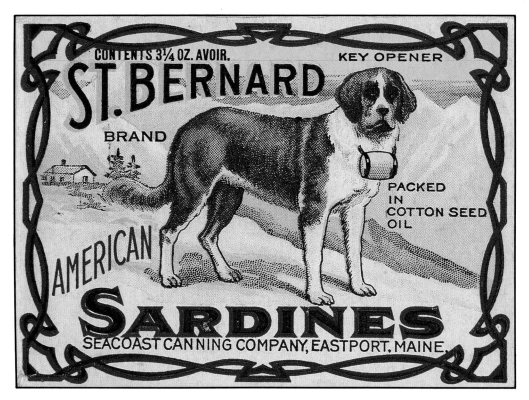

The Saint Bernard, named after the Saint Bernard Hospice in the Swiss Alps, is shown standing in a mountain scene on this product package from the 1920s. This breed became famous for rescuing mountain climbers who became stranded. The keg shown hanging around the dog's neck presumably held brandy or another liquid that would help sustain life in the threateningly fierce conditions of mountain climbing. Although the dog makes a striking illustration for the sardines box, why it was chosen to promote the product is not known. The Seacoast Canning Company was incorporated in 1914 but only remained in business a dozen years.

The July
25 Cents
American
Magazine

ollecting "scraps" was one of the most charming pastimes of yesteryear. Scraps are colorful die-cut paper figures that were sold by shops and fancy stationers, mostly during the 1800s. Because color printing was a novelty in these early years, people cherished scraps for their beauty and collected them in "scrapbooks." Most of the printing was done in England or Germany.

This hobby was at its peak in Europe during the Victorian era, and then the tradition came to America with the immigrants. Some of the most beautiful scraps were printed in the late 1800s during what is known as the "golden age of scraps." Greeting cards of the nineteenth century were usually handmade, and scraps were the main decoration. Stationery was also decorated with scraps, as were valentines, calling cards, keepsake boxes, and even large screens used as room dividers. Some chair backs and tables were adorned with scraps and covered with a coat of lacquer.

Interest in scrap collecting declined after Queen Victoria's death, and early into the twentieth century it all but ceased. Still, many lovely examples can be found.

The dog scraps on these pages show intricate beauty and amazing detail. Among other favorite subjects for scraps were many animals, such as cats and birds, soldiers of many lands, flowers and fruit clusters, cherubs, children, and castles.

These dressed-up pups were produced by Rafael Tuck & Sons Ltd. of England and printed in Germany ("Funny Dogs," Gigantic Relief No. 873, Artistic Series). "Relief" refers to the embossing that made the figures seem more lifelike. They were originally attached into one large sheet by paper tabs and the shields that identified the breeds.

OR THE ENGINE

C.B.Q. TABLETS

C.B.Q.

in Danger!

but no more so than you are when you neglect a cold.
You can be cured, as the little girl is being saved, by taking
HILL'S CASCARA BROMIDE QUININE
35 TABLETS 25 Cents.
MONEY REFUNDED IF NOT SATISFIED.

Sales promotion takes many different forms, but giving away calendars is a tried-and-true way of keeping the name of a product prominent in a household all year long. But in the late 1800s and early 1900s, it was companies such as W. H. Hill of Detroit, Michigan, that tested the theories of merchandising that are so easily accepted today. The theme of a dog saving a child from doom was so appealing when it was first used (*above*), that it was repeated on the company's 1904 calendar (*right*). CBQ, a patent medicine sold for relief of colds, coughs, and other ailments, is no longer made.

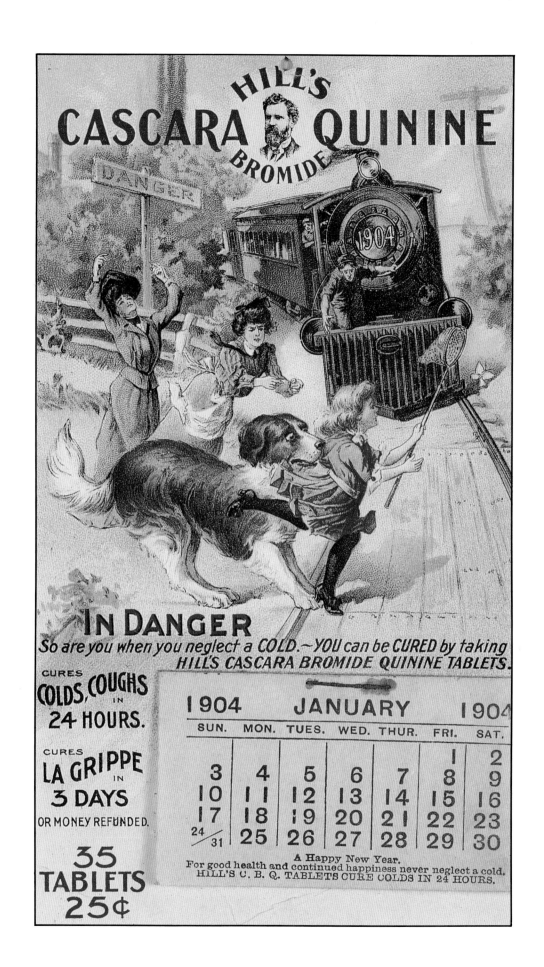

A charming cocker spaniel made a back-to-school statement for Texcel tape in the early 1950s. Although this countertop in-store sign looks three-dimensional, it's really a cleverly die-cut piece of cardboard. Texcel, a product of the Permacel Tape Corp., was discontinued when the company was sold in 1958.

It's unusual not to picture the product or a car in an advertisement for spark plugs! But the Champion Spark Plug Co. selected an identifiable and friendly symbol instead in this magazine ad from 1950. Along with spark plugs, Champion also produces automotive chemicals, filters, and cables.

A basset hound is the symbol for Hush Puppies® brand shoes. The Hush Puppies name can be traced to the 1950s, when the sales manager for the Wolverine Company first tasted fried corn dough balls called "hush puppies," a favorite of Southern cooking enthusiasts. He was told that farmers often fed hush puppies to their hungry dogs to quiet their barking. The name seemed a natural for the company's new line of casual shoes—because they were so comfortable they would ease the annoying aches of tired feet (or "barking dogs")!

Hush Puppies shoes were introduced in 1957 and became immediately successful. The basset hound has been present from the beginning, appearing in print advertisements and television commercials, as well as on the brand's shoe boxes. Today, there are even specialty shoe stores with the Hush Puppies name.

The Wolverine Company began in Grand Rapids, Michigan, in 1883 as the Hirth-Krause Co. G. A. Krause and his uncle, Fred Hirth, were experienced in the leather tanning trade and started a wholesale leather and shoe business. They soon expanded and built the first company shoe factory in Rockford, Michigan, in 1903, where Wolverine World Wide is still headquartered. The company—undoubtedly with the help of its strikingly different canine brand—is an international success story today.

Classic Hush Puppies.

We have all our favorites leather bound.

Casual Hush Puppies.

These comfortable leather shoes are as laid-back as a Saturday afternoon. Perfect for shopping, errands or just hanging out.

A basset hound has always figured prominently in Hush Puppies advertising. Hush Puppies are known the world over and, in the United States, brand recognition is nearly universal. One survey showed fully ninety-seven percent brand recognition among adults. At the left are some award-winning modern Hush Puppies ads.

Colorful labels were found on wooden fruit crates shipped across the country in the 1920s and 1930s. There were many thousands of brands, representing hundreds of growers and growers' associations. The Fido brand appeared on oranges and lemons in the 1930s as a companion to the now-defunct Orosi Foothills Citrus Association's Tom Cat brand. The Pic O Pac brand (*right, top*) was introduced by the Pinnacle Packing Co., Inc., around 1930 and continued through 1980. The dog image helped to convey that this fruit was "the pick of the litter." Today, Pinnacle Orchards is a successful mail order fruit company. Scotty's Best pears were named for a man, not the cute dog pictured on this fruit crate label (*right, bottom*)! Scotty was the nickname of Earl Griffith, who managed the Cedarwall Sales Co. warehouse for many years. Cedarwall was a fruit brokerage house for orchards, and Scotty's Best pears are no longer sold.

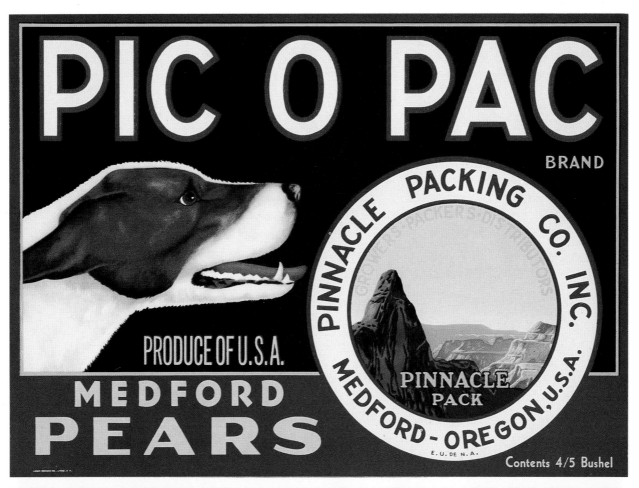

BEST PAL

A delicious Caramel, Cocoanut, Roasted Almonds and Milk Chocolate Confection.

Childhood is so much more fun when you share it with a best friend. That's the message from the maker of Best Pal candy bars, who wisely pictured an ideal friendship on the brand's box (*shown above*). Louis Glick founded the Euclid Candy Co. in Cleveland, Ohio, in 1925 and opened factories in Chicago; San Francisco; and Brooklyn, New York. Although the Cleveland branch closed in 1931, the other locations prospered under reorganization. Best Pal bars, made of "caramel, cocoanut, roasted almonds and milk chocolate," were produced at the company's San Francisco plant. The slogan "The Sensation of 1940" is printed on the side of the box. The Best Pal brand was made through the 1950s, but Euclid was sold in the early 1960s and, by 1972, all candy operations had ceased.

The charming image at the right was used to promote Post Toasties corn flakes in 1909–1911, both as a tin lithographed sign and in a printed advertisement. C. W. Post actually began his successful cereal-manufacturing career in 1891 as a patient in the Battle Creek Sanatorium run by the Kellogg family. An illness had caused Post to seek rest and rehabilitation, and, while hospitalized, he was served cereals created by Dr. John Kellogg. Upon recovery, Post experimented with making cereals of his own. He introduced Grape-Nuts (see pages 20–21) in 1898 and Post Toasties in 1904. Around the same time, W. K. Kellogg bought the rights to produce his brother's cereals—and thus was born another famous cereal company and competitor to Post. The Postum Cereal Co. combined with several other food manufacturers in the 1920s and became known as General Foods in 1929.

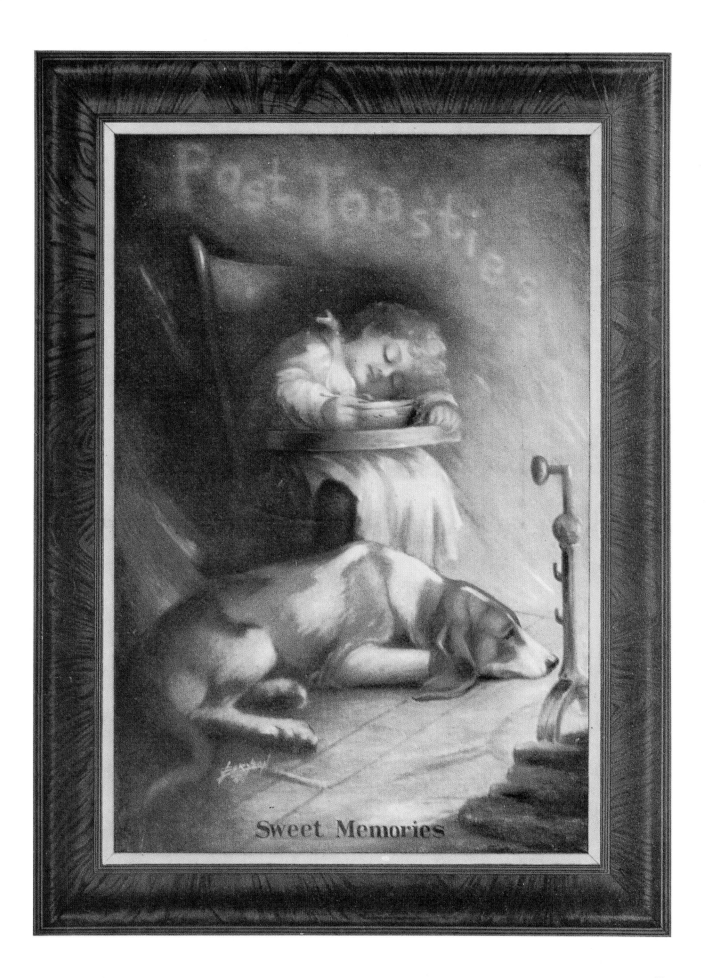

Sweet Memories

When it comes to pet care products, the name Sergeant's stands out as a leader. But Sergeant is more than a name—it was a real dog owned by the company's founder, Polk Miller, more than a hundred years ago. Miller was a Richmond, Virginia, pharmacist who created various remedies at his drugstore to treat his beloved dog. Encouraged by friends who had also tried his products for their pets, Miller began selling a line of pet care products at his pharmacy. And the rest is history. Sergeant's became part of the A. H. Robins Company in 1967 and currently has over 350 items in its pet care line, including products for dogs, cats, other small animals, birds, and even fish. The tin store display box shown below is from the 1940s and measures 14¼″ high × 15″ wide × 7″ deep. The colorful lithograph below is actually a printer's proof of a large window sign from the early 1950s.

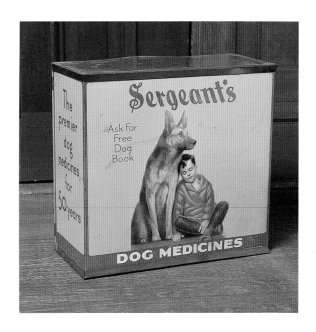

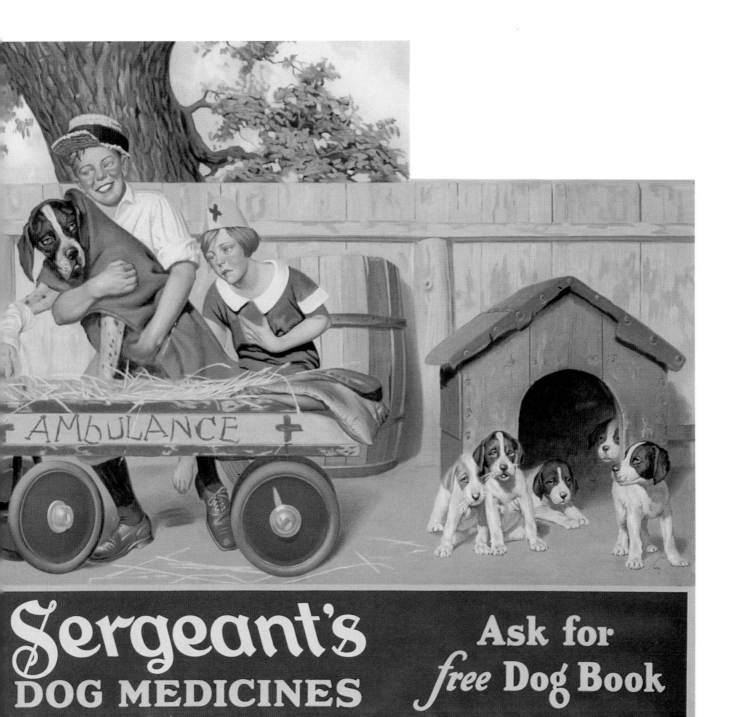

he top dog of the transportation industry is, undoubtedly, Greyhound. With the sleek image of a greyhound dog dashing across its side, the Greyhound bus is as much a part of America as apple pie.

Greyhound grew from the dream of Carl Eric Wickman, a Swedish immigrant who settled in Hibbing, Minnesota. With money he saved from working in the iron mines, he bought a Hupmobile auto dealership in 1913. When no one bought the top-of-the-line model, he bought it himself and began operating it as a workman's bus service, driving seven miners daily over the ten-mile distance between Hibbing and the mines. The cost was fifteen cents one-way or a quarter round-trip.

Over the years, Wickman bought many other local bus lines. His dream was to build a nationwide system so passengers could travel cross-country on a single ticket. During the 1920s, a number of bus companies purchased by Wickman had "Greyhound" in their name. Nobody knows who first selected the sleek canine to symbolize speed in travel, but by 1930, Wickman had changed all the names of his affiliated companies to Greyhound Lines.

Greyhound became a strong leader in excursion travel packages in 1933. While most of America was feeling the Great Depression, the company advertised nationwide to attract people to the World's Fair in Chicago. Greyhound reserved 2,000 hotel rooms and offered a bus ticket plus hotel accommodations for a single price. The promotion was wildly successful. Since then, millions of people have taken vacations and toured America by bus.

In 1957, the corporate logo came alive when "Lady Greyhound," a beautiful purebred, appeared on television and made hundreds of appearances wearing a jeweled tiara and collar!

Today, the well-known Greyhound symbol still accompanies thousands of travelers every day, gracing the sides and back of buses and appearing on bus station signs in large and small towns alike.

Painted and glazed porcelain-over-metal signs like the one on page 50 hung outside bus stations all across America in the 1930–1960 period. It measures 20″ × 36″. The promotional ink blotter shown below advertised Greyhound Vans. This division of the company operated nationwide from 1929 to 1973.

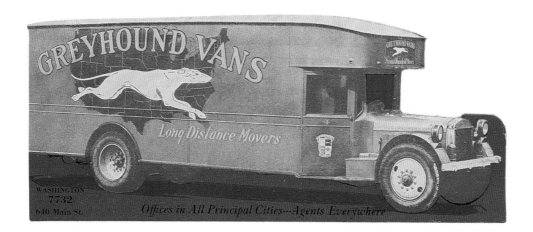

Use NIAGARA CORN STARCH,
Superior to all.

CHAMPION ST. BERNARD "OTHO"
WINNER OF 31 FIRST PRIZES.

Sharing life with a pet teaches children valuable lessons in getting along with others. And in return for friendship, pets are loving companions. Three typical child-and-pet scenes are depicted here. *Right:* An overly enthusiastic dog begs for a taste of dairy cocoa. The colorful lithographed paper sign in French from the late 1800s says this was "the best of all chocolate and cocoa products known," and it was available in all drugstores and groceries. Unfortunately, the company and product no longer exist. *Top left:* A beautiful child poses with a Maltese on this advertising card for Niagara Corn Starch. This product was produced in the 1880s by Wesp, Lautz Brothers & Co., Buffalo, New York, but is no longer made. *Bottom left:* Pearline was a powdered washing compound sold by the James Pyle Co. of New York in the late 1800s. In 1899, the brand was registered to The Hewitt Soap Co., which continued to produce Pearline until the late 1940s.

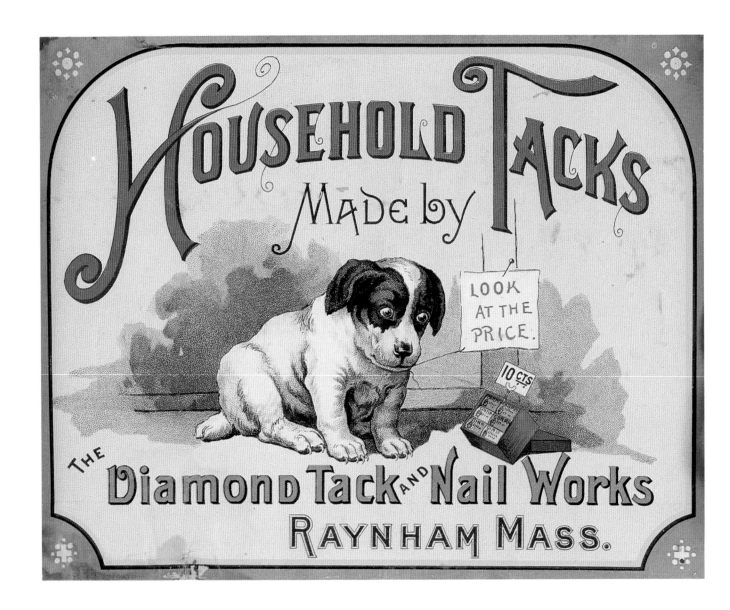

This cute pup wanted customers to look at the inexpensive price of Household Tacks back in the early 1900s. The image is on the inside lid label of a display box of twelve small tack boxes. When set out on a countertop or inside a display case, the dog was sure to be an attention-getter! The iron-rich town of Raynham, Massachusetts, was the site of the nation's first ironworks. The Diamond Tack and Nail Works was an early manufacturing company there, operating from 1909 until 1930. For some unknown reason, the illustration on the labels of all the individual tack boxes features two cats instead of the dog!

"THE 666 CLINIC"

The Monticello Drug Co. created a series of decorative promotional prints for pharmacists to give to their customers (ca. 1920s). Of course, product information was carried on the back, promoting Monticello's 666 liquid, tablets, and salve for use in treating colds, nausea, and malaria. This illustration was by Charles Twelvetrees, a well-known postcard and greeting card artist.

More than a half a century separates the two items shown below, but both were designed to encourage good habits for children. The card on the left is one of a series given to nineteenth-century children who regularly attended Sunday school. The Victorians recognized academic performance and attendance at church or school with various kinds of "Rewards of Merit." Sometimes these rewards were expensive pins made of gold, silver, or bronze. More often, rewards were made of paper or cardboard inscribed by the teacher, and students collected and saved them in scrapbooks. The back of this card carries a Bible lesson and quiz for December 26, 1897. It was printed by Harris, Jones & Co. of Providence, Rhode Island.

Coins could be placed in the basket carried by the faithful friend on the right. It's a die-cut bank, probably from the 1940s. It was a clever way to encourage saving money that would pay the cost of an insurance premium. The John Hancock Insurance Co. began in Boston, Massachusetts, late in 1862. It was named for one of the signers of the Declaration of Independence, a fitting affiliation for a company whose business was founded on the principle of providing financial independence for American families. The company's first claim was paid in 1863. Today, the company is one of the most well known in the world, providing a wide range of diversified insurance, real estate, and financial services.

Jackson Coon made a name for himself in the late nineteenth century and lives on today through this unusual advertising clock that bears his name. Coon was in the lumber business, operated a saw and grist mill, and later started a retail store. He was also the postmaster of Rockford, Michigan, during Grover Cleveland's presidential administrations (1885–1889 and 1893–1897)—the only Democrat to hold that post between 1871 and 1910. This heavy metal figural clock was of the style popular in the late 1800s and early 1900s. It is probably from the Spanish-American War era (1898), as the dog's collar is imprinted with "Victory" and the dog's stance and rider simulate a soldier-in-battle image. Why the dog was selected for the clock instead of a horse remains a mystery today.

"OUR TRUST"

VEGETINE THE GREAT BLOOD PURIFIER.

Testimonials praising the curative powers of Vegetine, an early patent medicine, livened up advertising for the product in the 1870s and 1880s. It was made from the juices of barks, roots, and herbs as early as 1851 by a Dr. Cummings in Boston. Twenty years later, when H. R. Stevens became the owner of this "great blood purifier," he wrapped each bottle in a box with a bright orange label and even created advertising cards featuring his dog, Major. Major was six years old and was said to be a "pure blood Newfoundland, very intelligent and faithful, a good watchdog and a great pet among children." The picture was lithographed from an oil painting. Like many patent medicines, Vegetine is no longer sold today.

Alf Loyal was one of the few men to bring dogs into the spotlight of the American circus. Circus audiences were more accustomed to watching clowns, daredevil stunt acts, and exotic wild animals. But Loyal's trained dogs, which sometimes performed with horses, not only appeared along with these other acts—they were featured on this colorful poster. It was quite an accomplishment for an act not generally considered unusual enough for top billing! The Ringling Brothers Circus began in 1884 in Baraboo, Wisconsin. In 1907, the Ringlings purchased the rival Barnum and Bailey Circus, but the two shows operated independently until 1919, when they were combined into one gigantic extravaganza. That year, the familiar slogan "The Greatest Show on Earth" was first used. Loyal and his dogs appeared for the Ringlings between 1911 and 1918 and for the combined shows in the 1920s and 1930s. The last appearance was in 1938.

veryone has fond memories of exchanging valentines with a "sweetheart" or of making valentines for family members as a school project. While you might ordinarily think of delicate lace and cupids when valentines are mentioned, a large number of twentieth-century valentines featured animals. And dogs were no exception!

On these pages, you'll see dressed-up dogs (a holdover from the popularity of dressed-up animals during the Victorian period), adorable puppies, recognizable breeds, and just cute "mutts." Most of these valentines were found in keepsake albums.

Valentines are named for Saint Valentine, an early Christian priest. In A.D. 496, Pope Gelasius set aside a day to honor Valentine, who had been put to death because he performed marriage ceremonies in defiance of the Emperor Claudius, who wanted men to remain single and to serve in the Roman army. The day has become a tribute to love and sweethearts that is symbolized by hearts and flowers.

Some of the most colorful valentines have been printed in Germany, England, and the United States. Dogs can be found on serious, sentimental, and comical cards. Some valentines were designed to stand up on easel backs. Others were die-cut with the image on the front and a blank back for a message. Some "mechanical" valentines were made so that when a part was moved, other parts also moved to slightly change the illustration. The dogs at the bottom of page 63 change expression when the paw is moved! Later twentieth-century valentines are of the more familiar single-fold type with a verse inside.

I like my milk for breakfast
And meat when I would dine;
And best of all, I like to spoon
With you, my Valentine.

The dog featured on this early advertising card is a hero! He foils a robbery attempt when he holds fast to the would-be thief's cuff. The card was made for the Weissinger & Bate Tobacco Co. of Louisville, Kentucky. The company began in 1870 as Bartlett and Weissinger, a wholesale tobacco business. Between 1874 and 1887, it was known as the Weissinger and Bate Tobacco Co. This type of advertising card is called a "metamorphic," because a story unfolds as the card is unfolded.

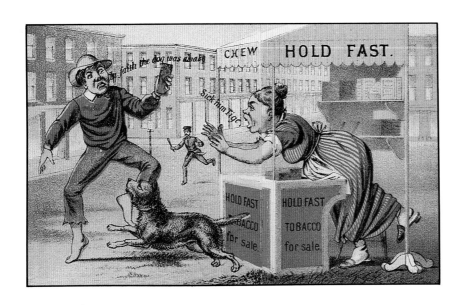

This Husky Service sign from a gasoline station (ca. 1940–1950) is a beautiful tribute to the Siberian husky, a breed that has a long history of friendship with man. The husky originated in northeast Asia and has been known as a faithful companion, hunter, and sled dog. The Husky Refining Company was formed in Wyoming in 1938. "Husky" was a brand already in use by the Park Refining Company, which became part of the new Husky company. The company slogan was "Husky Gets You Through." During World War II, Husky shipped as many as 15,000 barrels of fuel oil a day to the U.S. Navy. Today, Husky Oil, Ltd. is located in Canada, and its business is oil exploration, production, and refining. While the new Husky emblem (right) appears on service stations in Canada, there is, sadly, no longer any U.S. Husky presence.

A tin of Colman's dry mustard can be found today in virtually every cook's kitchen. But this familiar name has a long history. Jeremiah Colman discovered the special qualities of a particular type of mustard seed grown in the fields of Lincolnshire, England, in 1805. He put his name on the mustard he produced, and Colman's has been an international success story ever since. The rare tin container above was made in England, probably in the early years of the twentieth century. Titled "The Cavalier's Pals," the lid (*top photo*) and each side feature scenes of dogs. Colman's is now a product of Durkee French Foods, owned by the British firm of Reckitt & Colman.

Moyer's Oil of Gladness was an early patent medicine sold in general stores, such as the one in Centre Hall, Pennsylvania, owned by William Harter Meyer. Formerly a miller, Meyer went into the general mercantile business around 1890. Although the original calendar pad was later replaced with one from 1908, the calendar itself is probably from an earlier year. It's an interesting advertising piece because it blends the art style of the late-Victorian era (oversize dog with child) with newer Art Nouveau –style flowers and design elements. Like many patent medicines sold prior to the passage of the Pure Food and Drug Act in 1906, Moyer's contained a liberal dose of alcohol and opium—no doubt producing a "gladness" effect when administered!

The Yale University Bulldog graces these decorative tobacco tins for the Handsome Dan brand. The L. L. Stoddard Company was located in New Haven, Connecticut, home of Yale University, so the tins may have been created to feature the football team symbol and appeal to students or Yale alumni. Llewellyn L. Stoddard first operated a fruit store in New Haven, then a cigar store, during the 1880s and, later, a tobacco company until 1910.

Stylized art typical of the Art Deco era made a beautiful cover for *Woman's Home Companion* magazine in February 1931. The depiction of racing dogs symbolized the speed of an approaching winter storm. *Woman's Home Companion* magazine was one of the most well-respected women's magazines of this century, published between 1897 and 1957.

It's not unusual to find gun advertising featuring dogs, since hunting dogs have accompanied men on hunts for centuries. But it is unusual to find a woman featured along with the dog and gun. This sign from the Harrington and Richardson Company of Worcester, Massachusetts, dates to the late 1800s or early 1900s. Harrington and Richardson was one of the premier names in firearms at the time. Gilbert Harrington invented the first shell-ejecting handgun in 1871. By 1874, William Richardson had joined him in business. The company first added double-barreled shotguns to their line in 1880 and, in 1900, a single-barrel shotgun.

The cute puppies posed with the Winchester shotgun on this in-store dealer sign also appeared in magazine advertisements for Winchester repeating shotguns in 1904. The Winchester Repeating Arms Company was founded in 1866 in New Haven, Connecticut, by Oliver Winchester, who had previously been the owner of a successful shirtmaking company. He helped to change the course of the American firearms industry by producing repeating rifles and shotguns. The first Winchester shotgun was introduced in 1887. In 1931, Winchester became a division of the Olin Corp., manufacturer of industrial chemicals, metals, and various Winchester products, including ammunition.

Puppies and mischief just naturally seem to go together. But "puppy appeal" is hard to resist, so it's no wonder these two cigarette containers were saved for many years! The Temptation brand was produced by Cameron & Cameron, a Richmond, Virginia, company. Alex Cameron was a Scottish immigrant who was in Richmond both before and after the Civil War. He organized his first tobacco company in 1858, and Cameron & Cameron was formed in 1889. The company was dissolved in 1905. Puppies brand cigarettes was a product of the Alliance Cigarette Manufacturing Co. of New York. Originally a cigar manufacturing company, Alliance assumed "Cigarette" in its name in 1945. Alliance went out of business in 1948.

McCall's is familiar today as a successful women's magazine, but its beginnings were actually quite humble. James and Laura Belle McCall first published a "fashion" magazine in 1876 called *The Queen*. They had developed a line of dress patterns, and illustrations in *The Queen* helped promote sales of the patterns to women subscribers. Later, the name changed to *The Queen of Fashion*, and the *McCall's Magazine* name first was used in 1893. Over the years, *McCall's* added fiction, full-color fashion pages, and even full-length novels. The magazine has over five million readers today. The cover at the right is from 1914.

When there is no one to play with, a dog can really be counted on for love and companionship. And children are always fascinated by puppies. C. I. Hood & Co. made good use of this idea with the illustration on its Parlor Games book. Advertisers often created booklets as giveaways to keep their name within a customer's household. Hood's was a prolific advertiser of patent medicines, such as the sarsaparilla product advertised in this booklet that was said to purify the blood and restore energy.

ainy afternoons and wintertime pose challenges for children who must fill long hours staying indoors instead of playing outside. But today's children pass the time much differently than their parents or grandparents did. In fact, around the turn of the century and into the 1920s, children were usually quite resourceful in creating games and toys, since there were no televisions or radios for entertainment.

But there were wonderful commercially produced games and puzzles packaged in beautifully lithographed boxes that appealed both to children and their parents. Of these, board games have always been the most popular.

Usually, a route of some sort was printed on the game board, and each player, in turn, moved a token around the board; the distance of each move was determined by a spinner or dice throw. The first such game was created in 1840. The games most sought after by collectors today are those that date from the late 1800s through about 1930 or 1940.

Since children love dogs, and so many families over the years have kept dogs as pets, it's not surprising to find that dogs were a popular subject illustrated on game boxes, puzzle boxes, etc. On the next few pages, you'll see some lovely examples.

The Game of the North-Pole capitalized on the discovery of the North Pole on April 7, 1909, by explorers Robert Peary and Matthew Henson. Sled dogs accompanied the men on their journey, so they are, of course, featured on the cover. Game manufacturers often linked their games to current events to keep their product line interesting. This game was made for the English-speaking market by the J. W. Spear and Söhne Company in Germany and appeared in its 1909 catalog.

Many adults today have fond memories of having been met at the school bus stop by their dog, who was delighted to have a playmate for the rest of the day! From the style of clothing and the hoop being rolled along by the children, this game appears to be from the 1920s. Parker Brothers has been making children's games for over a century and offered Tiddledy Winks® from 1891–1968. Tiddledy Winks® is a game of skill in which small disks are flipped onto a scorecard or into a cup or compartments by pressing them on the edge with a larger disk.

This lithographed biscuit tin was offered in 1938 and 1939 by the W. & R. Jacob biscuit company of England. In the 1920s and 1930s, there was a great demand for decorative biscuit tins abroad. Many "novelty" items were created for use as children's toys after the biscuits were eaten. "Pongo" was described as "an intriguing and amusing enamelled tin" in Jacob's 1939 Christmas catalog. It came filled with iced biscuits (cookies), and its wheels turned so that it could be used as a child's pull-toy. To make it even more interesting, Jacob included an outer carton that looked like a dog kennel! W. & R. Jacob & Co. has been producing fine biscuits in Ireland and England since 1850 and, in 1982, joined the Nabisco Group Ltd.

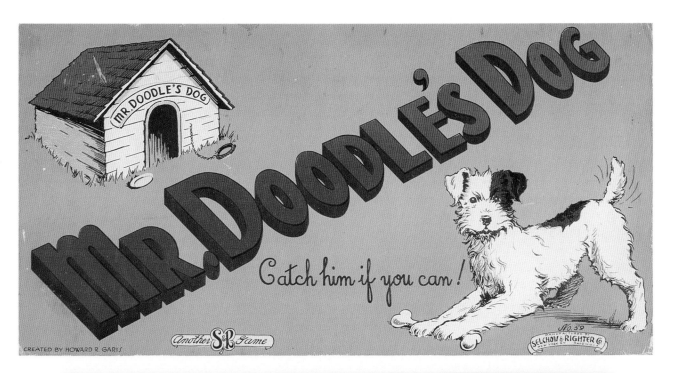

The object of the game shown above was for Mr. Doodle's dog to leave his dog house at the top of the game board, enter a home to get a bone, and bring it back to his dog house—all without being caught by a home owner along the route. A white metal dog represented the dog in the game. The top photo shows the box lid; the bottom photo displays the game board and spinner. Scampering dog graphics helped make this a lively pastime for the children of the 1930s and 1940s, when the game was available. It was made by the Selchow & Righter Co.

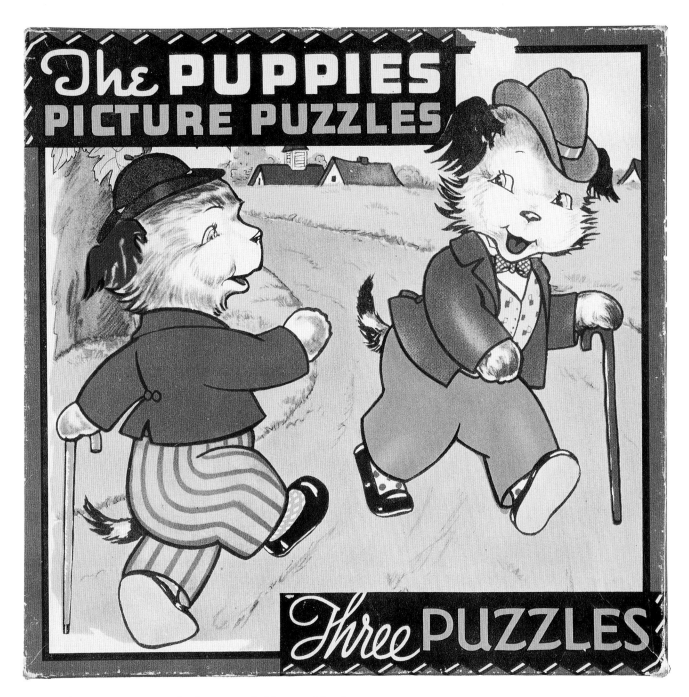

Over the years, jigsaw puzzles have provided hours of fun for
children. These cute puppies were created by the Saalfield Publishing
Co. of Akron, Ohio. There were three puzzles in the box—one
depicted the cover scene (*shown here*), one showed a dressed-up
doggie family, and one pictured an orange kitten! "The Puppies" was
one of a series of animal puzzle sets produced by Saalfield in the
1940s. The company was founded in 1909 and was best known for
publishing children's books, paper dolls, and "big little books" during
the 1930s and 1940s. Saalfield went out of business in 1979.

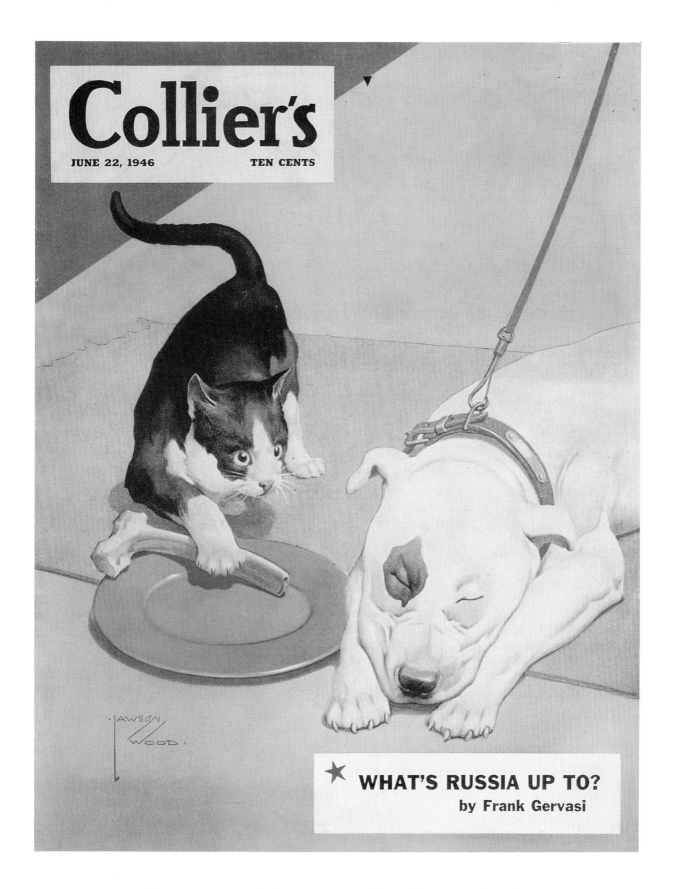

Comical covers were typical of *Collier's* magazine during the 1940s, and British artist Lawson Wood created a great number of them featuring animals. He is particularly well known for illustrations of chimps. *Collier's* began publication as a general-interest magazine in 1888, and the last issue appeared in 1957.

NATURE'S KINDERGARTEN.

A STANDARD SEWING MACHINE.
AND BUY
KEEP OFF THE GRASS

Be Jaber's the Children all scream wid delight
It's the illigant Soap that makes them so white

—USE—
CRANE'S
Family and Toilet Soap

When high-speed presses made color printing available and affordable in the late 1800s, enterprising printers sold companies on the idea of giving printed cards like these to customers. Of course, each carried an advertising message on the back. Lavine (*right*) was an all-purpose "washing, scrubbing and housecleaning" soap made by the Hartford Chemical Works of Hartford, Connecticut. Crane's (*above, right*) was sold as a family and toilet soap. The Standard Sewing Machine Co. of Cleveland, Ohio, selected a charming group of puppies and a school theme for their "Nature's Kindergarten" card (*above, left*). The first straight-stitch sewing machine patent was issued by the U.S. Patent Office in 1848, and by the time this advertising card appeared in the late 1800s, more than half a million sewing machines were in use. Standard machines are still sold today.

WOMAN'S HOME
Companion

DECEMBER 1937   TEN CENTS

ANNETTE BYRNE

CATHALEEN
& TOBEY

© THE CROWELL PUBLISHING COMPANY · PUBLISHERS OF THE AMERICAN MAGAZINE · COLLIER'S · THE COUNTRY HOME MAGAZINE · WOMAN'S HOME COMPANION

The "all-American" look of a child and her pet appeared on the cover of *Woman's Home Companion* in December 1937. The focus of this magazine during the 1930s was on the household, and it was purchased mostly by housewives who turned to its pages for practical advice. From its first issue in 1897 until its last in 1957, it delighted readers with a combination of lively and interesting articles.

81

35 Cents
$3.50 a Year

THE MAGAZINE FOR PLAYGOERS

JUNE, 1914
VOL. XIX NO. 160

THE THEATRE

(TITLE REG. U. S. PAT. OFF.)

The Theatre Magazine Co.,
8-10-12-14 West 38th St., N.Y.

MISS LAURETTE TAYLOR
in "Peg O' My Heart"

Many dogs love to ride in cars—and this *International Magazine* cover (ca. 1915) proves this was true even in the automobile's early days. This magazine was published by the International Tailoring Co. of Chicago, Illinois, and New York, which at the time was the largest manufacturer of made-to-measure men's suits. The magazine contained articles of general interest while heavily promoting the styles offered by the company. Jacob Reiss founded International in 1896, and the company is still family-owned. The Chicago factory building still stands, but the tailoring business ceased operations in 1952. Since the 1950s, the company, now known as the North American Reiss Corp., has manufactured structural foam and injection-molded components for the computer and telecommunications industries.

Theater enthusiasts found the beautiful illustration at the left on the cover of *The Theatre* magazine in June 1914. The featured actress, Laurette Taylor, was starring in a production of "Peg O' My Heart" and was also found endorsing a brand of hats in an advertisement inside this issue. *The Theatre* published critical reviews, articles about the theater, and profiles of professional actors from 1900 to 1931.

"I dare you!"

The candy with the hole . . . still only 5¢

FIVE FLAVOR LIFE SAVERS

Who could resist such a look? But the question one must ask is whether this cute basset hound is daring you to take his piece of candy or daring you to pass it by? This advertisement appeared in 1957. Life Savers candy was first made in 1912 when Clarence Crane came up with the idea of a hard candy mint to bolster lagging summer chocolate sales at his Cleveland, Ohio, candy factory. He hired a pill-maker to press the new candy into a circle with a hole in the middle to differentiate it from square-shaped European imports, and called it Life Savers (for obvious reasons). A New York advertising man then bought the rights to the candy and began marketing it nationwide. Today, in addition to the original mint variety, Nabisco Brands, Inc., the current owner of Life Savers, sells more than two dozen other flavors.

Mrs. Steven's candies were sold in decorative Art Deco–style tins like this one during the 1930s and 1940s. Julia Clark Steven was born in a log cabin. She began informally, selling fudge in a small Illinois town shortly after World War I, and then founded the Mrs. Steven Candy Company in 1921 in Chicago with just $1,000 in capital. The firm grew to employ more than 400 people, making hand-dipped candies that were sold in Mrs. Steven's Candy Shops in Chicago; Milwaukee, Wisconsin; and Indianapolis, Indiana, by the 1950s. When the company was sold in 1956, it was a $4 million-per-year business.

The Mascot brand of tobacco shows a
Chihuahua, one of the world's smallest dogs, as
its symbol. This pocket mirror is a good
example of an advertising item given away to
customers to promote a brand. It is made of
celluloid and was produced by the Whitehead &
Hoag Co., the premier producer of celluloid-
backed mirrors and advertising pin-back
buttons. This form of advertising was popular
from the 1890s through the 1920s. Mascot was
offered by the P. H. Mayo & Brother Tobacco
Co. of Richmond, Virginia. Peter H. Mayo came
from a family of tobacconists that had lost its
fortune in the Civil War. In 1866, he and his
brother William set up their own company in
Richmond, selling mostly to customers in New
England. The company was sold to the
Continental Tobacco Co. in the late 1890s.

Pocket tins of cigars were popular from around
1910 to the 1940s. This Scotty brand tin (*top,
right*) is unusual in that it shows the dog with a
cigar in its mouth! "Little" cigars were slightly
smaller than a regular-size cigarette. This tin
could hold ten cigars and still fit easily into a
jacket pocket.

The two interesting pocket tins at the right,
Terrier Brown Flake and Challenge Toasted Navy
Cut, allowed tobacco lovers to carry their
favorite brand with them wherever they went.
Terrier was produced by Cohen Weenen & Co.
of London. Challenge was made by the National
Tobacco Co., Ltd., of Port Ahuriri, New
Zealand, and distributed by the Lee Jobbing and
Commission Co. of New Haven, Connecticut.

The Flick and Flock tin was originally meant to contain five-cent cigars, but a paper label was later added to show a sale price of two for a nickel. They were made by the Roby Cigar Co. of Barnesville, Ohio. The Roby factory was destroyed by fire in 1921. Old Rover was a brand of chewing and smoking tobacco sold by the R. J. Reynolds Tobacco Co. The brand was originally owned by T. L. Vaughn and Co. but was purchased by Reynolds in 1900. The Mastiff brand gives tribute to one of the largest dogs. This chewing tobacco was produced by the J. B. Pace Tobacco Co. of Richmond, Virginia. James B. Pace entered the tobacco business in 1866 and operated his factory until 1903—the time when the American Tobacco Trust purchased many such companies. The Master Guard pail contained "stogies," a type of cigar that had originally been called "Conestoga," after the pioneers' Conestoga wagons, but the name was shortened by popular usage. Stogies were inexpensive (Master Guards sold three for a nickel) and long-lasting. Stogies originated in Pennsylvania and the upper Ohio River valley. Master Guard was introduced in 1914 by the Union American Cigar Co. of Pittsburgh, Pennsylvania, and continued by P. Lorillard & Co. of New York.

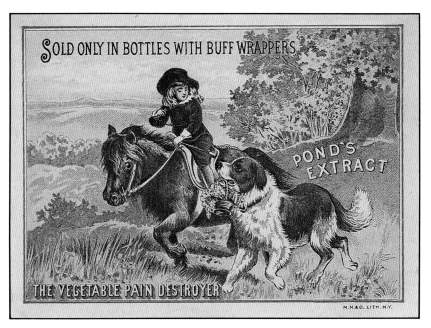

Dogs are so friendly that it's not unusual to find them in the company of other animals as well as people. A child exercises her pony and dog on this advertising card from the 1880s or 1890s. Pond's Extract was a patent medicine sold by the Pond's Extract Co. of New York as a remedy for a number of maladies, including sprains, tonsillitis, and diphtheria.

This innocent-looking pair probably just discovered the spilled milk—surely they didn't play a part in the accident that caused it! They appeared on this small tin (ca. 1905–1910) produced by Callard & Bowser, one of Britain's oldest candy companies. Daniel Callard and his brother-in-law, James Bowser, established the firm as a London bakery and confectionery in 1837. They introduced their "Butter-Scotch" candy in the late nineteenth century. Today, the Callard & Bowser Group still produces a wide variety of candies sold in Europe and the United States.

Manufacturers of all kinds of products in the late 1800s created advertising signs, such as this one for Velvet Tobacco, for use in stores where the product was sold. At least half a dozen companies marketed tobacco under the Velvet brand name at one time or another, but the most famous and successful was Liggett & Myers, which created the Velvet Joe character, Velvet's long-time spokesman. Although no longer produced, the Velvet brand now belongs to The Pinkerton Tobacco Company.

J. D. Larkin & Co., established in 1875, was the first company to provide premiums—usually colorfully printed cards of children or animals—inside the product package or separately, to be given away by the merchant. By the mid-1880s, the company offered larger premiums with large orders—even writing desks, chairs, and stoves! Eventually, a complete line of household products, including paint, perfumes, food specialties, and pharmaceuticals, became part of the Larkin line, and the company later diversified into making furniture and clothing. Like many other companies across the U.S., Larkin felt the effects of the Depression of the 1930s and never completely recovered. By 1940, the company had closed its doors forever.

The whippet, a breed known for its speed, was adopted by The New Home Sewing Machine Company to symbolize the fast speed at which its machines could operate. In fact, the whippet is the fastest domesticated animal for its weight. The dog appeared on advertising cards, like the ones shown here, which were given away to customers in the 1880s and 1890s. The whippet also appeared in a large oil painting that hung in the New Home executive offices in the early 1900s. The company began in Orange, Massachusetts, in 1860. The owners changed the name to The New Home Sewing Machine Company in 1882, to reflect the popularity of their "Home" and, subsequently, "New Home" sewing machines. The company was sold in 1930 and moved to Rockford, Illinois; in the 1960s, it became a subsidiary of the Janome Sewing Machine Co., Ltd. of Tokyo.

All four sides of this British biscuit tin feature adorable dogs. In addition to the Yorkshire terrier and fox terrier sides shown, the others pictured a Pomeranian and a King Charles spaniel. This 6½″ × 2¾″ × 2¾″ tin was offered by MacFarlane Lang & Co., Ltd. in the 1920s or 1930s. MacFarlane Lang had its beginnings in 1817 when James Lang opened a bakery in Glasgow, Scotland. His nephew, John MacFarlane, took over the business when Lang died in 1848, and MacFarlane's heirs retained ownership until 1948, when the company joined with McVitie & Price, Ltd. to become United Biscuits.

The calendar at the right suggests to fathers that they should be insured for the sake of their children. And this beautiful child and her pet made a winsome pair that could make parents smile all year long. The Prudential Insurance Co. of America, founded in 1875 by John Dryden as the Prudential Friendly Society in Newark, New Jersey, was intended to provide inexpensive life insurance for working-class individuals. Prudential is now the largest insurance company in America. When this calendar was produced, the company boasted of having more than $1.5 billion in life insurance in force; today, that figure tops $700 billion!

Animals and children helped the National Carbon Company, Inc., promote its Eveready flashlight batteries in the 1930s. Students of the famous illustrator Norman Rockwell were commissioned to create a series of whimsical scenes, such as the two shown here. The illustrations were incorporated into magazine advertisements and offered as 10″ × 14″ prints for ten cents—without the advertising wording. Large posters were also created to hang in dealers' stores. The Eveready Battery Company, Inc., traces its history to the American Electrical Novelty and Manufacturing Co., which held patents for commercial dry cell batteries as early as 1896. By 1898, flashlights were available, but they were sold primarily as toys. As the Eveready battery became popular, the company changed its name to match its best-selling product. Today, Eveready is owned by the Ralston Purina Company.

AN UNINVITED GUEST.

Hires' Rootbeer.

The wording on the back of this late 1800s card says that children like Hires' Rootbeer but "Fido, the pet Shepherd dog, is drinking it all up!" Charles E. Hires, a Philadelphia pharmacist, was on his honeymoon in 1870 when he was served a delicious drink made from roots, bark, and herbs. He worked for years to find just the right combination of flavors to sell at his drugstore's soda fountain. Then, in 1876, the samples of Hires' Rootbeer he gave away at the Centennial Exposition in Philadelphia created a nationwide demand, so he began packaging his drink as a dry extract to which water, sugar, and yeast had to be added. That package is advertised on the back of this card. In 1880, a liquid concentrate was created, followed in 1893 by the first bottled Hires' Rootbeer. More than a hundred years since its creation, Hires' is still a leading root beer (now owned by Crush International, Inc.).

ACKNOWLEDGMENTS

We would like to thank the following people who helped us create *The Dog Made Me Buy It!*:

Brandt Aymar, editor at Crown Publishers, Inc., for his continued enthusiasm and support, and *Jane Jordan Browne* for representing us. We are deeply grateful to *two collectors* who allowed us to select items from their outstanding collection of antique advertising for inclusion in our book. Although they wish to remain anonymous, we truly appreciate their tremendous contribution to the success of this project. Also, thanks to *Ken Kapson* for continuing to share with us his knowledge of history and popular culture, and for the time and energy spent helping us; *Susan B. Nicholson*, for her enthusiastic search for dogs to include in the book; *Louis Auslander*, president of the International Kennel Club of Chicago and chairman of the board of the American Kennel Club; the staffs of the National Tobacco Textile Museum and the Tobacco Merchants Association of the United States; and the dozens of libraries, historical societies, museums, and others across the country who assisted us.

We also wish to thank *Peter Basdeka* for his excellent and creative professional photography. All photos in this book are his work except for those taken by *Barry M. Sawyer*, who generously helped us take advantage of photo opportunities when they arose by taking on-location shots—shown on pp. 8, 12, 13, 30 (top), 33, 50, 55, 59, 65 (top), 70, 71, 73. The photo on p. 43 appears through the courtesy of Fallon McElligott.

A number of people were kind enough to make items available to us for photography. Our sincere appreciation to our *anonymous friends* for allowing us to photograph items on pp. 7, 10 (bottom), 11, 15, 17, 19 (bottom), 20, 23, 29, 30 (bottom), 31 (bottom), 34 (bottom), 46, 48 (left), 53, 57, 66, 68, 72, 75, 76, 86, 87, 88 (bottom), 89, 92; *Susan B. Nicholson* for items on pp. 6, 8, 25 (left), 26 (bottom), 36, 37, 52, various valentines (pp. 60–63), 73, 80 (bottom), 90; *Ken Kapson* for items on pp. 3, 4, 14, 16, 18, 21, 22, 26 (top), 27, 28, 30 (left), 32 (bottom), 33, 35, 38, 39, 58, 64, 74, 79, 80 (top), 82, 83, 85, 93, 95, 96; *Phil & Karol Atkinson* for items on pp. 70, 71; *Cy Gold*, p. 12; *Frank Knizek*, pp. 13, 65 (top); *Kim & Mary Kokles*, p. 30 (top); *Tom Fay*, p. 45 (bottom), *Robin R. Ward*, pp. 48 (right), 49; and *Larry Lubliner*, p. 59.

We also appreciate the cooperation of the many companies that gave us permission to reproduce their advertising: p. 3—Courtesy of Coats & Clark Inc.; p. 5—Reproduced with the permission of Reckitt & Colman plc; pp. 8, 9, 10, 11—Permission to use granted by Brown Group, Inc., St. Louis, Missouri. All other uses are strictly prohibited; p. 15—Jeyes Group Ltd.; pp. 18, 19—Photo courtesy of Thomson Consumer Electronics (RCA), Indianapolis; p. 20—Courtesy of Gillies Coffee Co., New York, NY 10012; p. 33—© 1988 Kuppenheimer; p. 40—Courtesy of Permacel, a Nitto Denko America Co.; p. 41—Courtesy of Champion Spark Plug Company; pp. 42, 43—Hush Puppies Footwear, Division of Wolverine World Wide, Inc.; p. 45—Used with permission of Pinnacle Orchards; pp. 48, 49—© A. H. Robins Consumer Products Division; p. 51—This advertisement is reproduced with the permission of The Greyhound Corporation, owner of the registered trademarks displayed therein and of the copyrights pertaining thereto. All rights reserved; p. 56—John Hancock Mutual Life Insurance Co. and Affiliated Companies, Boston, MA 02117; p. 59—Reproduced by permission of Ringling Bros.-Barnum & Bailey Combined Shows, Inc.; p. 65—Reproduced by permission of Husky Oil Ltd., p. 66—Used by permission of the Durkee-French Foods Division of Reckitt & Colman, Inc., and Reckitt & Colman plc; p. 70—Reproduced by permission of Winchester Div., Olin Corp.; p. 71—Harrington & Richardson is a trade name of Harrington & Richardson, Inc., an Ohio corporation. Use of this name without the express written permission of Harrington & Richardson, Inc., is prohibited; p. 73—Reprinted with permission from *McCall's* magazine. Copyright 1914 by The McCall Publishing Co., all rights reserved; p. 76—Tiddledy Winks® game equipment used with permission from Parker Brothers; copyright 1891; p. 84—Reprinted with permission of Nabisco Brands, Inc.; p. 88 (top)—Reproduced courtesy of Chesebrough-Pond's Inc., owner of the registered trademark POND'S; p. 88 (bottom)—The copyright of Smith Kendon Ltd. (Callard & Bowser Group) is acknowledged in accordance with United States law; p. 91—New Home and Light Running Dog; p. 92—Photo reproduced with kind permission of United Biscuits (UK) Limited; p. 96—© The Procter & Gamble Company. Used with permission.